MUMMIES AND TOMBS

CONTENTS

SALIMA IKRAM

Illustrations by Riham El Sherbini

HOOPOE BOOKS

MUMMIES

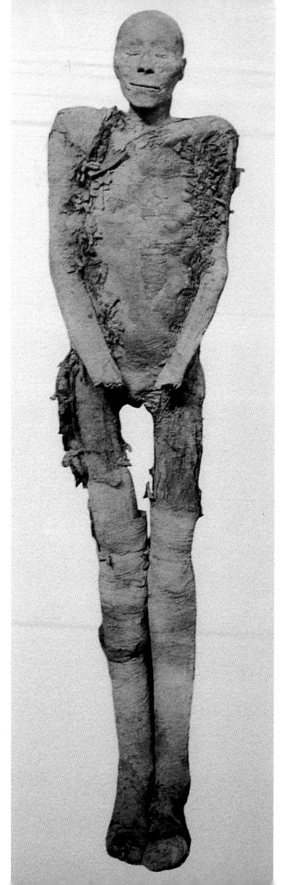

The ancient Egyptians believed in life after death. It seems they thought that in order to live forever the soul needed a body that would last forever, so they took a lot of trouble to preserve the body. Many of these preserved bodies, or mummies, still survive.

The Egyptians considered that the afterlife was very similar to the best of this life, so they provided the mummy with everything that it would need. They believed that through magic spells, everything placed in the tomb and written or drawn on the walls of tombs would come to life in the next world. They filled the tombs with objects and covered the walls with pictures and writings.

Right: Some Egyptologists think this mummy might be the pharaoh Tuthmoses I – his hands were broken off by robbers when they stole his jewellery.

How many different activities from the afterlife can you count in this painting from a tomb wall? What are they?

The word mummy comes from an Arabic word *moom*, which means wax or tar. It was once believed that this was used to make ancient Egyptian mummies because they were covered with a thick dark paste. However, we now know this paste was actually resin from trees such as juniper or pine. The ancient Egyptians themselves did not use the word mummy, but instead the word *sah*.

We know a lot about mummification from scientifically examining mummies that have been found. There are also some texts written by ancient Egyptians as well as by later Greek historians like Herodotus, which describe mummification in some detail.

The hieroglyph for a mummy

Egyptian tombs were usually robbed of their jewellery and furniture in ancient times, sometimes just after the burial. When the royal tombs in the Valley of the Kings were robbed the mummies of the pharaohs were moved and hidden for safety in another tomb at a place called Deir el-Bahri, south of the Valley of the Kings.

The mummies remained there safely for almost 2,800 years until the 1890s, when an Egyptian family that lived nearby discovered the tomb. The family started selling off the jewellery and boxes until the antiquities organisation found out and managed to catch the robbers. Finally the robbers, who had been fighting amongst themselves, confessed everything.

The antiquities police went to the tomb and in two days cleared all the mummies and their belongings. These were loaded onto a boat and taken down the Nile to Cairo where the mummies were to be stored in the museum. All along the river, from Luxor to Cairo, people lined the river bank. It was a strange journey. The village men fired their guns into the air to salute the mummified pharaohs as they passed, while the women made wailing cries as they still do today at funerals in the Egyptian countryside.

The antiquities organisation moving the mummies from their hiding place to take them to Cairo.

The idea of mummification probably came to the Egyptians very early in their history.

In the Pre-dynastic Period (before 2920 BC) the Egyptians used to bury their dead in shallow graves in the desert. In the graves they placed pots, beads and other objects that the dead person had used in life and might find useful in the afterlife.

The hot, dry desert sand dried out the body and preserved it perfectly as a natural mummy. This gave the Egyptians the idea of mummifying people.

Mummification became especially important when Egyptian tombs became more and more complicated. Now the dead person was no longer buried in the hot sand, but in a coffin and a sarcophagus that were put inside a stone tomb. A sarcophagus is a rectangular stone box in which the wooden coffin is placed.

The Egyptians probably started mummifying bodies during the Old Kingdom (2575-2134 BC). We do not know exactly when they started, because excavations keep giving us new information about ancient Egypt.

Left: A stone sarcophagus decorated with magic spells and pictures of gods who would protect the dead person. A pair of eyes was carved on one side so the mummy could look out of the sarcophagus at its tomb. (The lid has been raised to allow visitors to see inside.)

Below: This body, known as "Ginger" because of the colour of his hair, was naturally dried and preserved by the desert sand. Ginger was buried in the Pre-Dynastic Period in a shallow grave with some pots to use in the afterlife. Mummies like Ginger might have given the Egyptians the idea of mummification.

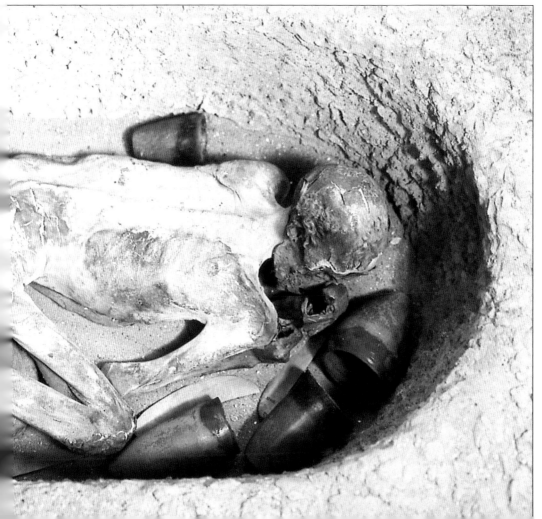

Above: Anubis was the god of mummification. Here he is preparing the final wrappings of a mummy which is lying on a funeral bed.

There was more than one way of mummifying bodies and gradually different techniques were developed. The people who prepared the mummies are called embalmers. The most common method they used was this: the first step was to remove the brain. (The ancient Egyptians did not know what the brain does and thought it was unimportant.) A narrow chisel was pushed through a nostril and into the brain area. Then a thin metal tool was used to mash the brain up. After a day or two the mash could be poured and pulled out of the nostrils with a hooked instrument. Sometimes it helped to turn the body face down so that the brain could more easily drain out of the nostrils. The empty skull was then often stuffed with linen and melted resin was poured in through the nostrils.

Next a cut was made in the left side of the body. The intestines, liver, lungs and stomach were taken out so that they would not rot inside. The heart was left in place as the ancient Egyptians believed that intelligence, thoughts and feelings came from the heart and therefore it was very necessary in the afterlife.

The inside of the body was then washed out with a natron solution or palm wine, and dried using solid natron.

Natron is a mixture of salt and soda and is found in Wadi Natrun near Cairo. Mummies could be made with common salt if natron was unavailable. Natron and salt both act like hot sand: they remove all the moisture from the body, leaving it dry and well preserved.

Right: Embalmers mummified bodies in special workshops away from the villages. They needed lots of air, water, natron and sunlight to do their work properly.

Above: The embalmers placed amulets in the wrappings of the body while they worked.
Right: Tutankhamun's gold mask, showing him wearing a kind of headdress called a
Nemes crown. The holes in the ears would once have held earrings.

After this, the body was laid on a stone slab and covered in
powdered natron for 40 days or more, completely removing the
moisture from the flesh. Sometimes bits of the body like fingers or
toes would fall off if they became very dry. When that happened,
the embalmers used pieces of wood and linen to make artificial
fingers and toes so that the mummy had all its limbs for use in
the afterlife. In order to make sure the mummy did not lose
fingers or toes after it had been wrapped, gold finger and toe tips
were sometimes placed on the mummy's hands and feet.

Once the body was dry, it was cleaned out and filled with more
natron, linen and various spices including myrrh, and sometimes
with sawdust and lichen too. It was then sewn up with linen thread.
Resins were often added to the inside and outside of the body.

After the body was completely dry it was removed from the natron and wrapped in linen bandages. Protective amulets were hidden in the wrappings. A big cloth was wrapped around the body and held in place by linen strips.

Often a mask of the dead person's face was put over the head of the wrapped mummy. This mask was made of painted cartonnage, which is a mixture of linen, plaster and glue – a little like *papier maché*. Rich people also had gold leaf on their masks or, if they were a pharaoh like Tutankhamun, had masks made of solid gold.

The lungs, liver, stomach and intestines, which had been taken out of the body, were also covered with natron, washed with natron and wine, and then completely dried with natron and coated with resin. Each of these four organs was wrapped to look like a tiny mummy, sometimes even with its own mask. These packages were placed in four pots called canopic jars.

Above: The lids of some canopic jars have animal and human heads. Each head represents a different god who looked after a particular organ. In front of the four jars lies a hawk-mummy.

The four jars were then put in a square box – the canopic chest – which was placed at the foot of the body in the tomb.

In some periods of Egyptian history, the embalmers tried to make the body look very life-like. They stuffed the body with sawdust and linen to fill out the shape. They put in false eyes made of painted stone so that the mummy would look awake. They also painted the body with reddish-yellow paint so that the skin did not look too much like dried leather.

Right :
The mummy of Nodjmet, with a well preserved wig and eyes made of stone.

13

After the body had been wrapped it was placed in a coffin – or several coffins that went inside each other – and then put into the stone sarcophagus. Egyptologists think it took about 70 days to prepare a mummy properly, but some mummies took longer than others. Forty of these days were needed to dry out the body and 30 more to wrap it. As you can see, it took a lot of work to make a mummy and it was very expensive. Not everyone could afford to be mummified in the traditional way. Poorer people often did not have their inner organs removed. The outside of the body was just packed with salt. Often the bodies of the poor were not washed with wine or filled with expensive spices like myrrh.

The poorest of all were just wrapped up in rags and buried in a hole in the desert, inside a reed mat or a simple wooden box, as was done in the Pre-Dynastic Period.

Right. A poor burial. The body was wrapped in a mat or linen shroud and placed in the tomb pit with a few objects.

14

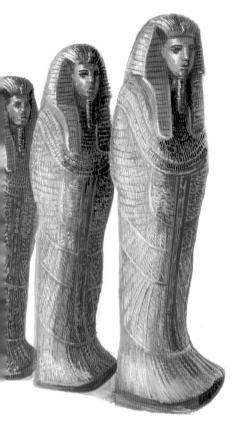

Left: This type of coffin is known as a *rishi* coffin because of the feather decoration (*rish* is the Arabic word for feathers).

In mediaeval Europe people thought that mummies could be used as medicine. The mummies were sometimes eaten as a cure for problems with bones and blood. Later, mummies were also used for fires in winter and as fuel for steam trains. These are some of the reasons why there are so few mummies left in Egypt now.

The Egyptians did not mummify only people. They also left mummified pieces of meat and poultry in the tomb as food for the afterlife. Egyptians also mummified whole animals: some because they were pets, like gazelles or cats, others because they were sacred and were supposed to have the spirit of a certain god in them. These were all buried in special graveyards. For example, the Apis bull was worshipped because it was believed to contain the spirit of the god Ptah. Only one sacred bull lived at any one time, and when it died it was carefully mummified and placed in an enormous sarcophagus. Then the priests had to find a new Apis bull, which they chose for its special markings such as white hairs in its tail.

Below: Mummified pieces of meat: the shoulder of a cow, a duck, some geese and a pigeon.

Other kinds of animals were given as offerings to particular gods. The baboon and the ibis – a type of bird – were sacred to Thoth, the god of writing. Hundreds of thousands of these were mummified and put into tombs. Cats were sacred to the cat-goddess Bastet and they were also mummified. Falcons and sometimes even scarab beetles were mummified and offered to the sun-god.

Right: Mummified cats were popular offerings to the goddess Bastet. Much later, in the 19th century, thousands and thousands of these cat mummies were discovered by visitors to Egypt. There were so many that sailors used the mummies as ballast or weight for their ships when they returned to Europe. There they sold the mummies to farmers to be used as fertiliser. However, when people began to get sick after eating food from the farmers' fields, this unpleasant trade came to an end.

FUNERALS

After the mummification the ancient Egyptians took the body to be buried. All the family and friends of the dead person would gather together and form a procession. The mummy would be carried in front, with priests singing and waving incense in front of and behind it. Next came the dead person's family, followed by friends. Sometimes the family would hire professional mourners who wailed and threw dust on their heads to show how much the family would miss the dead person. At the end of the procession came people carrying all the things to be put in the tomb.

The funeral procession of a noblewoman. The coffin, lying on a boat, is being dragged from the river to the tomb on a wooden sledge.

At the tomb the priests would perform a ceremony called the Opening of the Mouth, in front of the mummy. We still do not know exactly what happened during this ceremony but we do know that it was intended to help the mummy to breathe, eat, sleep and enjoy a complete life in the afterlife. During this ceremony a special tool was held to the mouth of the mummy, which was supposed magically to help the mummy come back to life.

Above: The Opening of the Mouth ceremony with a funerary priest wearing an Anubis mask.

After the Opening of the Mouth ceremony the mummy would be put into the coffins and sarcophagus which were then placed inside the tomb with all the furniture, baskets, scrolls, food, jewellery, weapons and make-up that were necessary for the afterlife. Several statues of the dead person would also be put into the tomb. These were made for the soul of the dead person to live inside, in case anything serious happened to the mummy.

The dead person's relatives and friends would cry as the body was placed in the tomb. Then, according to evidence in texts and ancient remains of food found near tombs, everyone attended a big banquet with lots of food and drink. They feasted and remembered the dead person. It was a party for the soul of the dead person. It is thought that the ancient Egyptians believed that the dead person's soul sat with them at this party.

In Ireland people have funeral parties called "wakes", with speeches about the dead person as well as singing, dancing and food. In modern Egypt some people take picnics to the cemetery on Fridays and on holy days so that they can eat beside their ancestors. In Mexico there are also big picnics and parties at tombs, when food and drink is shared among relatives and friends.

Right: Anubis brings the dead person to be judged by Osiris, while Thoth takes notes. Ammit waits next to the scales.

The Egyptians believed that the dead person's soul would travel to the afterlife where the heart of the dead person would be weighed against the "feather of truth" or *maat*. Maat was the goddess of truth and in the ancient Egyptian language the word *maat* also meant truth or justice. Maat's special symbol was a feather. When a dead person was judged, the heart was placed on one side of a pair of scales and the *maat* feather on the other side. If the scales balanced it meant that the dead person had lived a good life without lying, stealing or killing anyone. In this case, the god of the afterlife – Osiris – would grant eternal life.

However, if the scales did not balance and the heart was heavier, this meant that the dead person had lived a bad life. He would be punished and eaten by the monster Ammit, who was part-lion, part-hippo and part-crocodile. Ammit had very sharp teeth, stood next to the scales that weighed the heart and was always ready for a good meal.

TOMBS

The earliest tombs in Egypt were pits dug in the hard gravel that lies underneath the desert sand. However, the Egyptians soon started to build complicated tombs of several different types. Shaft tombs were very popular, as they are very easy and inexpensive to make. They are deep, narrow pits dug straight down into the ground. At the bottom of each pit is a room in which the body is buried.

Sometimes shaft tombs had more than one room at the bottom. Often, if the person was not wealthy enough to have the walls decorated, or if the rock was not of a good enough quality, then small wooden models showing activities from everyday life were put into these tombs.

Right. The tomb chamber was protected by a door made of soild stone

The *mastaba* was another type of tomb, consisting of a rectangular building containing lots of rooms and looking something like a house. The rooms were carved and painted with scenes from the person's life and from nature, as well as scenes of people bringing offerings of food and clothes to the dead person. The mummy was buried under the building, at the bottom of a very deep shaft.

A cutaway view of a *mastaba* tomb, with a view of the complete *mastaba* at the top

The ancient Egyptians thought of the *mastaba* as a house for the dead person's soul, and the first *mastabas* had the same kind of rooms that were found in houses, including toilets! Some of the most beautiful *mastabas* are found at Saqqara near Cairo.

Right: Mastaba tombs come in all sizes. Some have several rooms inside while others have one or two. The earliest *mastabas* had no rooms at all, just a place where offerings were placed.

The word *mastaba* comes from an Arabic word meaning bench. These tombs are called *mastabas* because they look like the mud-brick benches outside houses in Egyptian villages today.

The pyramids at Giza, outside Cairo. These are the largest tombs ever to have been built.

Another type of tomb is the pyramid. Only pharaohs and their queens were buried in these huge monuments. Pyramids were plain on the outside and had very little decoration inside. Sometimes the burial chamber inside the pyramid was covered with religious writings called Pyramid Texts. These were magic spells to make sure that the king arrived in the afterlife and enjoyed himself there. Pyramid Texts were first carved onto the pyramid of the pharaoh Unas during the Old Kingdom.

A magic spell from the Pyramid Texts says:

> *Oho! Oho! Rise up, O King!*
> *Take your head,*
> *Collect your bones,*
> *Gather your limbs,*
> *Shake the earth from yourself.*
> *Take your bread and your beer,*
> *Go to the gate.*
> *The gatekeeper comes and takes you into heaven.*
> *All rejoice at your coming,*
> *You are set before the spirits,*
> *You are an ever-enduring star.*

Pyramids were used to bury pharaohs throughout the Old and Middle Kingdoms. After that time the Egyptians chose other methods to bury their kings, since the pyramids were so often robbed. The remains of almost a hundred pyramids have survived in Egypt and others can be found to the south, in Sudan.

The most common type of tomb found in Egypt is the rock-cut tomb, which was carved into the side of a mountain. The tomb consists of two or three rooms that are painted with scenes of the person's life and of people bringing offerings to the dead person. The body itself is buried at the bottom of a shaft inside the tomb. Some rock-cut tombs, like those in the Valley of the Kings in Luxor, are very deep. Others, like those at Beni Hassan, are shallow. Some tombs had large entrances to look like the fronts of houses.

Above: The entrance to a rock-cut tomb at Beni Hassan, near El Minya. In ancient times, wealthy families appointed guards to watch over their relatives' tombs. (At the time it was built, it would not have had an iron fence.)

Some royal rock-cut tombs had tiny entrances that were covered with stone so that robbers could not break in and steal the things needed by the dead person in the afterlife. However, the robbers must have been very clever because most of the tombs in Egypt have been robbed. In the New Kingdom almost everyone, including pharaohs, was buried in rock-cut tombs. In their own tombs, pharaohs carved protective spells from the Book of the Dead or the Book of Gates. These protective spells were similar to the Pyramid Texts.

A priest or several priests were in charge of wealthy tombs. They guarded the tomb, and made sure that it was clean and that every day some offerings of food and drink were given to the tomb-owner.

Of course, the offerings were never actually eaten by the tomb-owner's soul. They were put in front of the statue of the dead person or the false door, and a prayer was said, giving the food to the soul. After that the priest himself would eat the food.

Right: A false door. This was a huge piece of stone carved and painted to look like a wooden door, and positioned inside or outside the tomb. The soul of the mummy was supposed to come out through this door to collect the offerings left for it or to listen to the prayers said to it. The hieroglyphs carved on the door give the name and titles of the deceased.

Later, after the funeral, relatives would come to visit the tomb and pray to the dead person. If they wanted the dead person to ask the gods for help, they might write letters to the dead person telling him what they needed. They would leave the letters at the tomb and hope that their dead relative would do something for them in the afterlife.

Sometimes people would just come to the tomb to talk to the dead person because they believed that the person's soul could hear them and would enjoy their company and news of the family.

Tombs were so beautifully decorated that people often went to visit cemeteries, especially in the Old Kingdom. They would go from tomb to tomb, admiring the decorations and looking for ideas to use on their own tombs.

A family visit to a rock-cut tomb

The cemetery at Giza has been used as a burial ground from the time of the first great pharaohs until the present day. In the background lies the Sphinx and the ancient tombs. In the foreground is the modern cemetery.

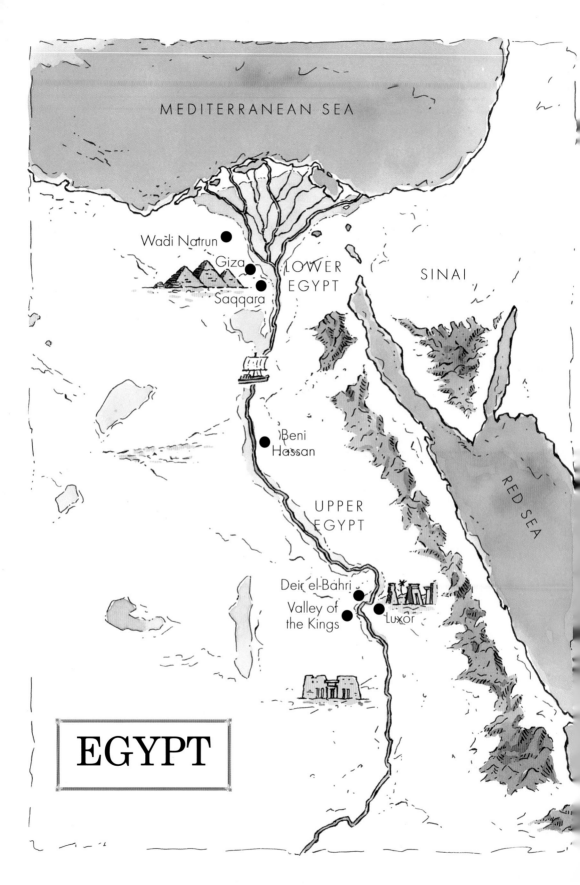

MEDITERRANEAN SEA

Wadi Natrun ●

Giza ●

● LOWER
Saqqara EGYPT

SINAI

● Beni
Hassan

UPPER
EGYPT

RED SEA

Deir el-Bahri ●
Valley of ●
the Kings ● Luxor

EGYPT

Glossary

afterlife   life after death

amulet   a small piece of jewellery used to protect people from harm

coffin   the box (usually made of wood) in which a dead body is placed

embalm   to treat a dead body in order to preserve it

Middle Kingdom   the period from 2040 to 1640 BC

New Kingdom   the period from 1550 to 1070 BC

Old Kingdom   the period from 2575 to 2134 BC

Pre-Dynastic Period the period from approximately 5500 to 3050 BC

sarcophagus   *(plural: sarcophagi)* a large outer coffin made of stone

---

Index

Photo credits